Amazing
Magic Tricks

DAVE BROWN & PAUL REEVE

DK

DORLING KINDERSLEY
LONDON • NEW YORK • STUTTGART

DK

A Dorling Kindersley Book

For Anna Brown and Gemma Hancock

Project Editor Helen Drew
Designer Cheryl Telfer
Production Louise Barratt
Managing Editor Jane Yorke
Managing Art Editor Gillian Allan
U.S. Editor Camela Decaire

Photography Dave King

Additional photography
Andy Crawford
Tim Ridley

First American Edition, 1995
2 4 6 8 10 9 7 5 3 1

Published in the United States by
Dorling Kindersley Publishing, Inc., 95 Madison Avenue
New York, New York 10016

Library of Congress Cataloging-in-Publication Data

Brown, Dave
  Amazing magic tricks / by Dave Brown and Paul Reeeve.
  -- 1st American ed.
      p.   cm.
  ISBN 1-56458-877-7
  1. Tricks--Juvenile literature. 2. Conjuring--Juvenile literature.
  [1. Magic Tricks] I. Reeve, Paul. II Title.
  GV 1548.B766 1995
  793.8--dc20   94-34863
                                                         CIP
                                                         AC

Dorling Kindersley would like to thank Rintje Howe for jacket design and
Jonathan Buckley, Jane Horne, Chris Scollen, Tim Button, and Adrienne Hutchison
for their help in producing this book. Dorling Kindersley would also like to give
special thanks to the following for appearing in this book: Gayle Atkinson,
Ebru Djemal, Arran Hall, Daniel Lawrence, Richard Lygo, Amy Morris,
Lian Ng, Daniel Regan, Tebedge Ricketts, and Samantha Thompson.

Illustrations by Coral Mula and Adrienne Hutchinson

Color reproduction by Colourscan, Singapore
Printed and bound in Italy by L.E.G.O.

CONTENTS

TRICKS BY PICTURES

Amazing Magic Tricks shows you how to prepare and perform astonishing magic tricks. The magic props are made from everyday materials and step-by-step photographs and simple instructions tell you exactly what to do. Speech boxes suggest lines to say to your audience, too. On the opposite page is a list of things to remember when using this book, and below are the points to look for on each page when preparing and performing the tricks.

How to use this book

The things you need
The things to collect for each magic trick are shown life-size to help you check that you have everything you need.

Equipment
Illustrated checklists show you the tools you will need to have ready before you start to make a magic prop.

Blue construction boxes
Step-by-step photographs in blue boxes show you how to make the magic props. Clear instructions tell you what to do.

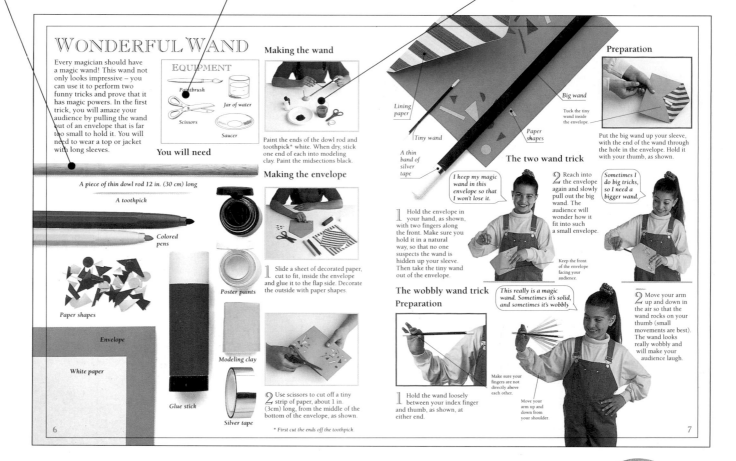

Things to remember

1. Read through all the instructions before you begin to make a prop or perform a trick, and gather together everything you will need.

2. Wear an apron when you are using glue or paint.

3. Be very careful when using scissors and sharp knives. Do not use them unless an adult is there to help you.

4. You must use dark-colored materials when they are shown for a prop. If you don't, it will be harder to fool your audience with the prop.

5. Put everything away when you have finished and clean up any mess.

6. You will need to practice every trick before you perform it. Look on page 48 for lots of tips on performing tricks.

Purple performance boxes
Things that you must do secretly during the performance of a trick are shown in purple boxes.

Red preparation boxes
Things that you must do in secret before you perform each trick are shown in red boxes.

Performance steps
Step-by-step photographs and clear instructions show you how to perform a trick. Speech boxes suggest what to say.

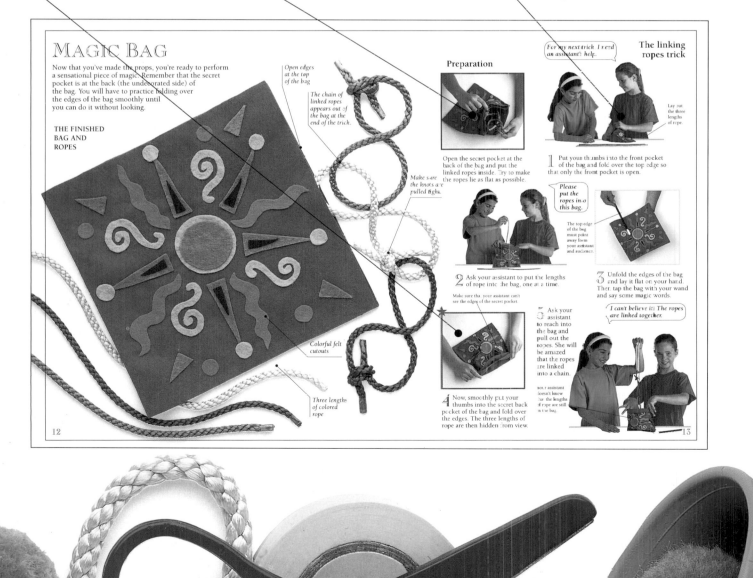

MAGIC BAG

Now that you've made the props, you're ready to perform a sensational piece of magic. Remember that the secret pocket is at the back (the undecorated side) of the bag. You will have to practice folding over the edges of the bag smoothly until you can do it without looking.

THE FINISHED BAG AND ROPES

Colorful felt cutouts

Three lengths of colored rope

Open edges at the top of the bag

The chain of linked ropes appears out of the bag at the end of the trick.

Make sure the knots are pulled tight.

Preparation

Open the secret pocket at the back of the bag and put the linked ropes inside. Try to make the ropes lie as flat as possible.

For my next trick I need an assistant's help.

The linking ropes trick

Lay out the three lengths of rope.

1. Put your thumbs into the front pocket of the bag and fold over the top edge so that only the front pocket is open.

Please put the ropes into this bag.

The top edge of the bag must point away from your assistant and audience.

2. Ask your assistant to put the lengths of rope into the bag, one at a time.

Make sure that your assistant can't see the edges of the secret pocket.

3. Unfold the edges of the bag and lay it flat on your hand. Then tap the bag with your wand and say some magic words.

4. Now, smoothly put your thumbs into the secret back pocket of the bag and fold over the edges. The three lengths of rope are then hidden from view.

5. Ask your assistant to reach into the bag and pull out the ropes. She will be amazed that the ropes are linked into a chain.

I can't believe it! The ropes are linked together.

Your assistant doesn't know that the lengths of rope are still in the bag.

12   13

WONDERFUL WAND

Every magician should have a magic wand! This wand not only looks impressive – you can use it to perform two funny tricks and prove that it has magic powers. In the first trick, you will amaze your audience by pulling the wand out of an envelope that is far too small to hold it. You will need to wear a top or jacket with long sleeves.

EQUIPMENT

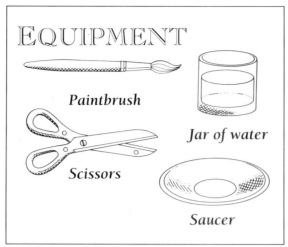

Paintbrush

Jar of water

Scissors

Saucer

You will need

A piece of thin dowl rod 12 in. (30 cm) long

A toothpick

Colored pens

Poster paints

Paper shapes

Modeling clay

Envelope

Glue stick

White paper

Silver tape

Making the wand

Paint the ends of the dowl rod and toothpick* white. When dry, stick one end of each into modeling clay. Paint the midsections black.

Making the envelope

1 Slide a sheet of decorated paper, cut to fit, inside the envelope and glue it to the flap side. Decorate the outside with paper shapes.

2 Use scissors to cut off a tiny strip of paper, about 1 in. (3 cm) long, from the middle of the bottom of the envelope, as shown.

* First cut the ends off the toothpick.

6

Lining paper

Tiny wand

A thin band of silver tape

Big wand

Paper shapes

Preparation

Tuck the tiny wand inside the envelope.

Put the big wand up your sleeve, with the end of the wand through the hole in the envelope. Hold it with your thumb, as shown.

The two wand trick

I keep my magic wand in this envelope so that I won't lose it.

1 Hold the envelope in your hand, as shown, with two fingers along the front. Make sure you hold it in a natural way, so that no one suspects the wand is hidden up your sleeve. Then take the tiny wand out of the envelope.

2 Reach into the envelope again and slowly pull out the big wand. The audience will wonder how it fit into such a small envelope.

Sometimes I do big tricks, so I need a bigger wand.

Keep the front of the envelope facing your audience.

The wobbly wand trick
Preparation

This really is a magic wand. Sometimes it's solid, and sometimes it's wobbly.

2 Move your arm up and down in the air so that the wand rocks on your thumb (small movements are best). The wand looks really wobbly and will make your audience laugh.

Make sure your fingers are not directly above each other.

Move your arm up and down from your shoulder.

1 Hold the wand loosely between your index finger and thumb, as shown, at either end.

7

VANISHING COIN

There's a very simple secret to some of the best tricks – a false bottom. Borrow a coin from someone in your audience and then, using the secret, make it vanish right before their eyes! Don't worry though, before the owner gets angry, you can make it reappear just as fast.

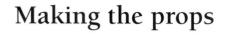

EQUIPMENT

Scissors

Tape

Pencil

You will need

Glue

Star stickers

A coin
(A thin coin works best.)

Silver and red shiny tape

Moon and star sequins

Thick yellow paper

Blue paper

A clear plastic cup

1 To make the tube, cut out a rectangle of thick paper wide enough to wrap around the cup. Tape it together and decorate it.

2 To make the mat, cut out a big rectangle of blue paper. Create an edge with tape and decorate the corners with stars and sequins.

3 Draw around the top of the cup on another sheet of blue paper. Cut out the circle. Glue it to the top of the cup. Trim the edges.

Silver
tape

Magician's
mat

**THE FINISHED
PROPS**

The coin trick

Cup with secret
paper circle

Sequined
tube

Red shiny tape

Do you know that your coin is a magic coin? Watch!

1 Position the tube and cup on the mat, as shown, before your audience arrives. When you are ready, ask someone for a coin.

This trick works best in the dark, so I'll cover the cup with the tube ...

2 Put the coin down in the center of the mat. Then pick up the tube and place it over the top of the plastic cup.

... and put them both over the coin.

3 Grip the cup through the tube and place it over the coin. Be very careful to tilt the bottom of the tube toward you.*

Look! The coin has vanished into thin air!

4 Wave your hand over the tube and say some magic words. Lift off the tube, leaving the cup over the coin.

* This keeps the audience from seeing the paper stuck to the top of the cup.

But don't worry – it will come back just as quickly.

5 To bring the coin back, put the tube over the cup and wave your hand over the top again, saying the magic words.

6 Then lift the tube and cup together to reveal the coin.

Here's your coin. Thank you for lending it to me. I'm sure you'll make it disappear soon!

Don't let the audience see the cup.

9

LINKUP!

In this trick, you will make three pieces of rope magically link together with just a wave of your wand. The trick lies in a secret pocket at the back of the bag that the audience doesn't know about. You can find out how to make the bag below, then turn the page to find out how to perform this incredible trick.

You will need

Tape

Three squares of dark felt for the bag

Strong glue

Three 2 ft. (60 cm) lengths of different colored rope

EQUIPMENT

Scissors

Ruler

Felt-tip or ballpoint pen

Making the bag

Glue all three squares of dark felt together, but only along three edges.*

Decorating the bag

1 Draw some shapes on the back of pieces of colored fabric. You will need to use a felt-tip or ballpoint pen for this.

*This makes a bag with a front pocket and a secret back pocket, both of which open at the top edge.

Squares of colored felt or other
fabric for decorating the bag

Magic wand
(see pages 6-7)

Preparing the ropes

2 When you have drawn lots
of shapes, cut them out. Turn
the shapes over so that you can't
see the pen marks on the fabric.

3 Arrange your shapes on the
the front of the bag. When
you are happy with your design,
glue the shapes to the bag.

Cut each rope into two 12 in. (30
cm) lengths, and tape around the
ends. Knot three different colored
ropes together to make a chain.

11

MAGIC BAG

Now that you've made the props, you're ready to perform a sensational piece of magic. Remember that the secret pocket is at the back (the undecorated side) of the bag. You will have to practice folding over the edges of the bag smoothly until you can do it without looking.

THE FINISHED BAG AND ROPES

Open edges at the top of the bag

The chain of linked ropes appears out of the bag at the end of the trick.

Colorful felt cutouts

Three lengths of colored rope

Preparation

Open the secret pocket at the back of the bag and put the linked ropes inside. Try to make the ropes lie as flat as possible.

Make sure the knots are pulled tight.

For my next trick, I need an assistant's help.

Lay out the three lengths of rope.

1 Put your thumbs into the front pocket of the bag and fold over the top edge so that only the front pocket is open.

Please put the ropes into this bag.

2 Ask your assistant to put the lengths of rope into the bag, one at a time.

The top edge of the bag must point away from your assistant and audience.

3 Unfold the edges of the bag and lay it flat on your hand. Then tap the bag with your wand and say some magic words.

Make sure that your assistant can't see the edges of the secret pocket.

4 Now, smoothly put your thumbs into the secret back pocket of the bag and fold over the edges. The three lengths of rope are then hidden from view.

5 Ask your assistant to reach into the bag and pull out the ropes. She will be amazed that the ropes are linked into a chain.

I can't believe it! The ropes are linked together.

Your assistant doesn't know that the lengths of rope are still in the bag.

13

CUPS AND BALLS

Here you can learn the oldest illusion in the world. Magicians have been performing with cups and balls for thousands of years – you will use pom-poms and make them pass magically through cups. Finally, one pom-pom will appear on the hand of a spectator! The secret lies in using an unseen "extra" ball, which the audience never knows about.

  You will need opaque cups that stack with a gap of at least 1 in. (3 cm) between the bottom of each cup, so that a pom-pom ball can hide between any two cups without the audience guessing that it is there.

You will need

Lots of star sequins

Three styrofoam cups
(Make sure that the open top of each cup is smaller than the back of your hand.)

Glue

Making the pom-poms

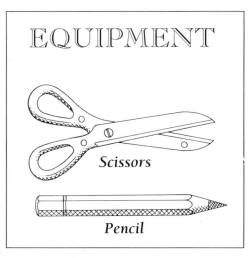

1 Draw around the bottom of a cup eight times on poster board, then around a coin in the middle of each circle. Cut the rings out.

2 Take two rings and wind a small ball of yarn around and around them, as shown, until the ring hole is filled in.*

*If you run out of yarn in the middle of a pom-pom, just start winding with a new length of yarn.

14

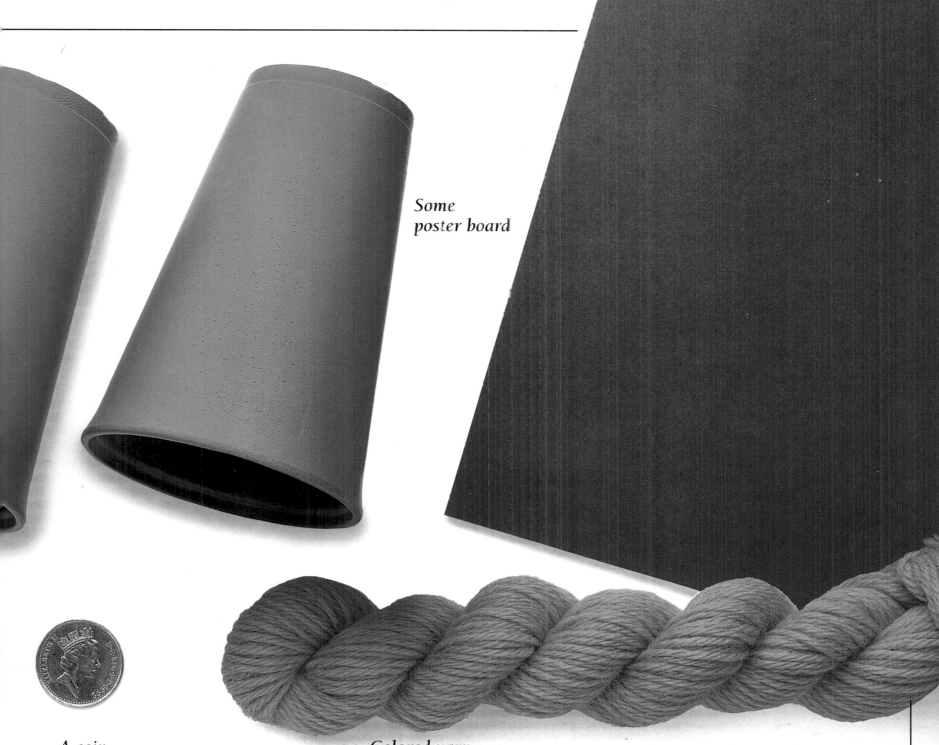

Some poster board

A coin

Colored yarn

Decorating the cups

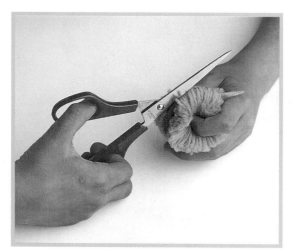

3 Next, slide the lower blade of your scissors between the two rings and cut the yarn all around the rings, as shown.

**Trim the pom-poms until each one fits easily inside the bottom of each cup.*

4 Put a piece of yarn in between the rings and tie a tight knot. Then pull off the rings and trim the pom-pom into a ball.**

5 To make the magician's cups, glue lots of star sequins all over the sides of the three cups, as shown.

15

Hide-And-Seek

This trick will make you look very skillful, yet it is really quite simple. Just follow the instructions closely and practice the trick until you can do all the moves smoothly. You must be able to turn the cups upside down quickly and smoothly, so that the secret ball can't fall out. Then you will be able to fool everyone with a piece of magic that is performed by the world's finest magicians.

Three star-spangled cups
Four trimmed pom-pom balls

The cups and balls trick

Preparation

Place three of the balls on the table, stack the cups, and put the secret fourth ball into the bottom of the middle cup, as shown.

This is the oldest magic trick in the world. It uses three cups and three balls. Now watch very closely ...

1 Take the bottom cup off the stack, smoothly turn its open end toward you, and then place it upside down behind the first ball.

Turn the open end of the cup toward you.

2 Take the middle cup (with the hidden ball), and smoothly turn it upside down, as shown in step 1, behind the middle ball.

3 Put the last cup behind the remaining ball. Then place the middle ball on top of the middle cup.

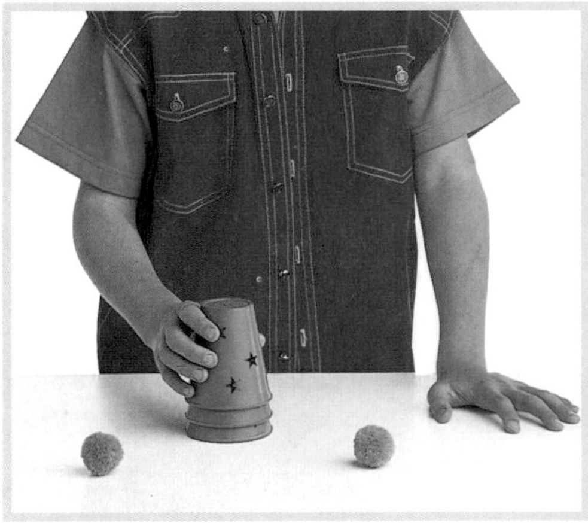

4 Stack one cup on top of the middle cup (this traps the ball between the cups). Then place the third cup on the stack.

When I tap the cups, the ball will jump magically into the bottom cup.
There is still a ball hidden in the middle cup of the stack.

5 Tap the cups with your hand, and lift the stack to show that the ball has passed through the bottom cup.

Remember to turn
the open end of the
cup toward you.

6 Starting with the bottom cup,
smoothly put the cups down
one at a time, placing the second
cup over the middle ball.

At this point there are two
balls under the bottom cup.

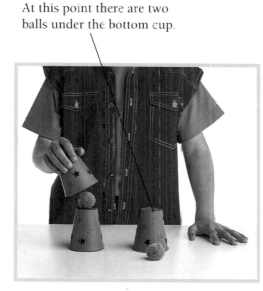

7 Once again, put a ball on
top of the middle cup. Then
cover it by stacking the other
two cups on top. Tap the top cup.

*Now there
are two
balls under
the cup!*

8 Then lift the stack to reveal
that there are two balls under
the bottom cup – a second ball
has joined the first!

*I'll need an
assistant
for the next
part of the
trick.*

9 Call for an assistant and ask
her to put her hand flat on the
table. Pick up the stack again, then
put the bottom cup on the table.

*Hold the
cup down
firmly with
your finger.*

10 Put the second cup (with
the hidden ball) on the back
of your assistant's hand.* Ask her
to press down firmly on the cup.

11 Put the single ball on top
of one cup and then cover
it with the spare cup, as shown.
Then tap the top cup.

*Look! An invisible
ball. Watch as I
throw it under the
cup on your hand.*

12 Lift the stack to reveal an
"invisible" ball. Pretend
to pick up the invisible ball and
throw it under your assistant's cup.

*Your assistant will not feel the ball on
the back of her hand.*

13 Ask your
assistant to
lift the cup from
the back of her
hand. She will
be amazed to see
that the last ball
has magically
appeared on top
of her hand.

*I don't
believe it!*

17

Colorful Clown

If you have ever tried to color in a picture, you know how long it can take. Wouldn't it be great if you could do it by magic? Well, this trick shows just that – a sad, colorless clown is put into an envelope, and emerges later on colored-in and happy. The method is very simple. All you need is some cardboard and two envelopes with secret pockets.

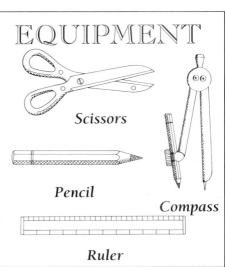

EQUIPMENT

Scissors

Pencil

Compass

Ruler

You will need

Colored pens

Shiny gold tape

Star stickers

Paper to match the envelopes (for the secret pockets)

Two large envelopes

White cardboard

Yellow poster board

What to do

1 Cut two rectangles of paper just smaller than the envelopes. Cut a window in the front of each envelope. Put a rectangle in each envelope to make a secret pocket.

2 For a stand, fold a poster-board strip in half and cut a notch in each end. Cut four rectangles of cardboard to fit in the envelopes. Color a side of each card the same.

3 Draw a clown on the blank side of two cards.* Draw four circles on the other two. Color in the happy clown and one set of circles.

* Draw one happy clown and one sad clown.

Frame each window with gold tape.

The backs of the cards can be seen through the window.

Envelope

Star sticker

The coloring trick
Preparation

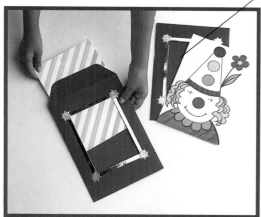

Put the card with blank circles into the **front** pocket of one envelope, as shown. Put the happy clown in the **front** of the other envelope.*

The audience will think the secret pocket is the back of the envelope.

This clown is sad because his life is so colorless.

Envelope containing the happy clown

Envelope containing the blank circles

1 Put the envelopes on the stands so that their backs face the audience. Show the audience the sad clown and the colored circles.

Let's see if we can cheer him up.

2 Put the sad clown in the **back** of the envelope that has the happy clown in it.* Put the circles in the **back** of the other envelope.

Now I'll say the magic words: Hey Presto!

Look! The colors have disappeared from this picture ...

... and they've appeared on the clown. Look how happy it's made him!

4 Turn the envelopes around and put them on the stands. Wave your hand over the envelopes and say some magic words.

* Remember which envelope contains the clown and which contains the circles.

5 Take the card with the blank circles from the front pocket of one envelope. Show the audience the colorless circles.

6 Take the colored clown out of the front pocket of the other envelope and show his happy face to the audience.

19

CUP THROUGH THE TABLE

This wonderful piece of magic uses a skill called misdirection (distracting the audience's attention from what is really going on). You must be seated at a table, but make sure nobody is watching from behind or beside you. Tell your audience that you will make a coin pass through a solid table by covering it with a plastic cup. Things don't go according to plan, and in the end it is the cup that passes through the table, not the coin! This trick is great fun to perform because your audience is expecting one thing to happen – but ends up getting a big surprise.

Plastic cup

Yellow tape

"Suns" made from 2 stars and a round sequin

You will need

Colored sequins

Yellow tape

Any coin

A square of colored paper big enough to cover the cup

Magic wand (See pages 6-7)

Glue

The table trick

I will now make this coin pass through the table.

To make the magic work, I have to cover the cup. Watch carefully.

1 Lay out your wand, paper, coin, and cup on the table in front of you. Then pick up the cup and place it upside down over the coin.

2 Place the piece of paper on top of the cup. Then, with both hands, scrunch the paper firmly around the cup.

3 Lift the paper and the cup to reveal the coin. Make sure that you grip the paper firmly, or the cup will drop out of your hand.

Now the coin has gone through the table. The hard part is to bring it back.

Look, it's back! You don't believe it? I'll do it again.

Pointing at the coin distracts the audience's attention from what you are really doing.

4 Still holding the cup and the paper firmly, put them back over the coin. Tap the top of the paper with your wand.

5 Lift the cup. Point and look at the coin (the misdirection). Meanwhile, move the cup to the edge of the table.

6 Rest your hand on the table, and let the cup fall onto your lap. The paper will keep the shape of the cup.

Don't lift the paper too high or the audience will see that there is nothing inside.

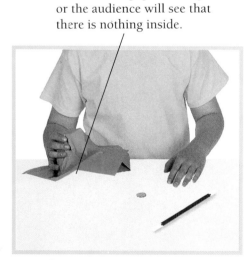

This time, I'll give the coin a hand.

9 Act puzzled for a few seconds, then lift the paper to show the coin. Finally reach under the table and bring the cup into view.

Oh! I think I need more practice!

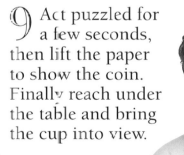

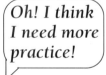

7 Cover the coin with the paper. Hold it carefully so that the audience thinks that the cup is still inside.

8 Using the palm of your hand smash the paper flat against the table. The noise will startle the audience.

COIN JOURNEY

In this trick, a coin disappears from the hand of a friend and reappears in a small, sealed box that has been in full view of the audience.

You will need to wear something with a pocket that is big enough to hold a matchbox and a secret coin slide. Pinning the slide to the inside of your pocket makes the trick easier to perform and ensures that your box and slide remain hidden.

You will need

Sequins and star stickers

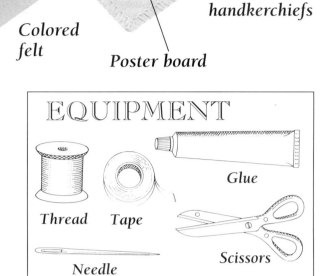

Two handkerchiefs

Colored felt

Poster board

EQUIPMENT

Thread   **Tape**   **Glue**

Needle   **Scissors**

Safety pin

Rubber bands

A matchbox

Cotton swabs   **2 coins**

Cut the ends off the cotton swabs.

Making the props

1 To make the tiny bag, cut a 1½ x 4½ in.(4 x 12 cm) strip of felt. Fold it in half and sew up the two long sides.

2 Cut a square from the corner of a handkerchief. Put a coin in a corner of another handkerchief, and sew the square over the top.*

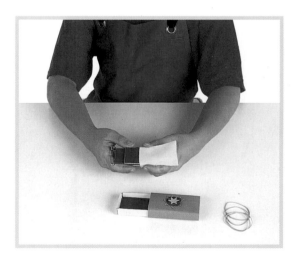

3 For the slide, cut two strips of poster board 1 x 2½ in.(3 x 6.5 cm). Glue cotton swab stems along the long sides of one strip.

4 Trim ½ in.(1 cm) from the end of the other strip. Glue it onto the stems on the first strip. Tape a safety pin to the slide's open end.

5 Finally, push the slide into the bag. Then put them both into the open box and slide the box closed. Stretch on the rubber bands.

*We have used red thread, rather than thread that matches the handkerchief, to show you how to make this prop.

22

Open end of the slide

Make sure no one can see the prop.

Rubber bands

THE FINISHED PROPS

The coin trick
Preparation

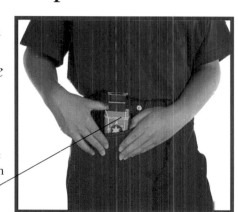

I'm going to make your coin disappear. But mark it, in case it ever turns up again.

Put the prop out of sight in your pocket, with the slide pointing upward. Then pin it to the back of your pocket.

1 Ask a friend to mark a coin with a felt-tip pen. Then pick up the handkerchief by the corner with the secret coin in it.

I'll cover the coin with the handkerchief.

Don't let your friend see the patch.

Hold the coin firmly.

Don't let anyone see the coin in your hand.

Oh! I forgot the box.

2 Put the marked coin on top of the secret coin. Then cover them with the handkerchief. Let the marked coin fall into your palm.

3 Give your friend the secret coin to hold. As he grips it, reach into your pocket and drop the marked coin down the slide.

4 Push the matchbox down and off the slide. Take the box from your pocket and put it on the table.

When I count to three, the coin will vanish. 1-2-3!

Since you've lost your coin, you can have the contents of this box instead. Oh! It is your coin!

5 Count slowly to three and then suddenly pull the handkerchief out of your friend's hand. He will wonder how the coin disappeared.

6 Ask your friend to open up the box and look inside. Take out the bag and tip the coin into the hand of your amazed friend.

23

ANTIGRAVITY SPECTACULAR

You can make the impossible happen with this astonishing piece of magic. Two clear plastic cups will defy gravity and remain attached to a book when it is turned upside down! Colorful silk scarves make the effect of the trick even more magical. The ingenious secret lies in two beads sewn into one corner of an apparently ordinary handkerchief that is wrapped around the book.

Two silk scarves

You will need

Two clear plastic cups

What to do

EQUIPMENT

Needle

Scissors

Thread

Pen

A book with a hard cover

Choose two beads and thread that are the same color as the handkerchief.

Put your thumb on one corner of the handkerchief and mark a dot on each side of your thumb. Sew a bead over each of the marks you have made.*

A large handkerchief

** Your thumb **must** fit **tightly** between the two beads. If the beads are loose, resew them closer together.*

Upside-down trick

> *These cups can float upside down in midair.*

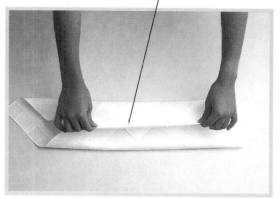

The two beads are hidden under the fold here.

1 Place the handkerchief on the table, and fold the beaded corner into the middle. Pick up the opposite corner and fold it toward you, as shown.

2 Fold the folded edges of the handkerchief together, as shown. The beads should be in the middle of the folded handkerchief.

> *You think it's impossible? First, I'll wrap a handkerchief around this book.*

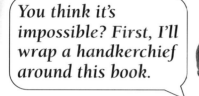

3 Place the handkerchief across the cover of the book. Then, lift up the cover and tuck the ends inside, as shown.

> *Then I'll put the cups and scarves on the book.*

4 Tuck a scarf into a cup, and put it upside down on the handkerchief, over a bead. Do the same with the other scarf and cup.

You should be able to feel the cups pressing against the beads.

5 Place your thumb between the cups and your fingers under the book, so that you are holding it firmly.

> *It's not impossible to turn everything upside down ...*

Put a hand on top of the cups to keep them in place.

6 Turn everything upside down, as shown. Then slowly remove your hand from underneath the cups.

> *... but this is impossible!*

7 Very slowly pull the scarves out from inside the cups, one at a time. And listen to your audience gasp with surprise!

25

HOUDINI ESCAPE

Houdini was a famous escape artist. He would be trapped in handcuffs and chains, inside padlocked boxes or cages, and yet he always managed to free himself. In this trick, you can make a strip of poster board, locked in a cage with a paper fastener, perform a staggering escape, right under the noses of your audience.

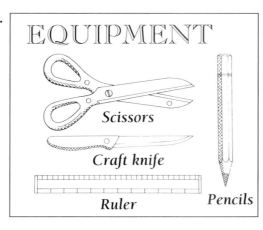

EQUIPMENT

Scissors

Craft knife

Ruler　*Pencils*

You will need

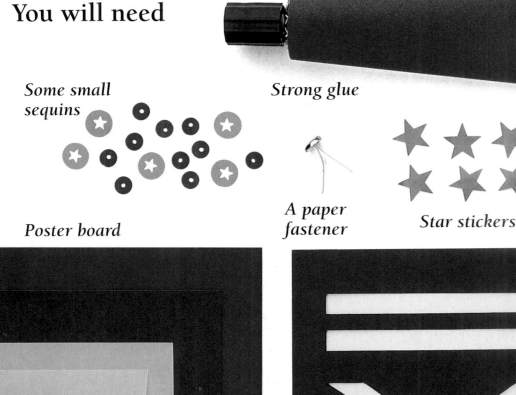

Some small sequins

Strong glue

A paper fastener

Star stickers

Poster board

Tracing paper

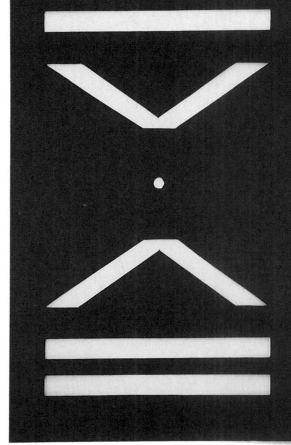

Template for the cage

What to do

1 To make the cage, trace the blue template at the bottom of this page twice onto yellow poster board. Cut both pieces out.*

2 Decorate the cage pieces with sequins and stars. Then glue the two pieces of the cage together along the long edges.

3 Cut a strip of blue poster board that can slide easily into the cage. Cut a hole in the middle that is bigger than the fastener top.

* Ask an adult to cut out the cage slots with a craft knife.

26

THE FINISHED PROP

Star sticker

The escape trick

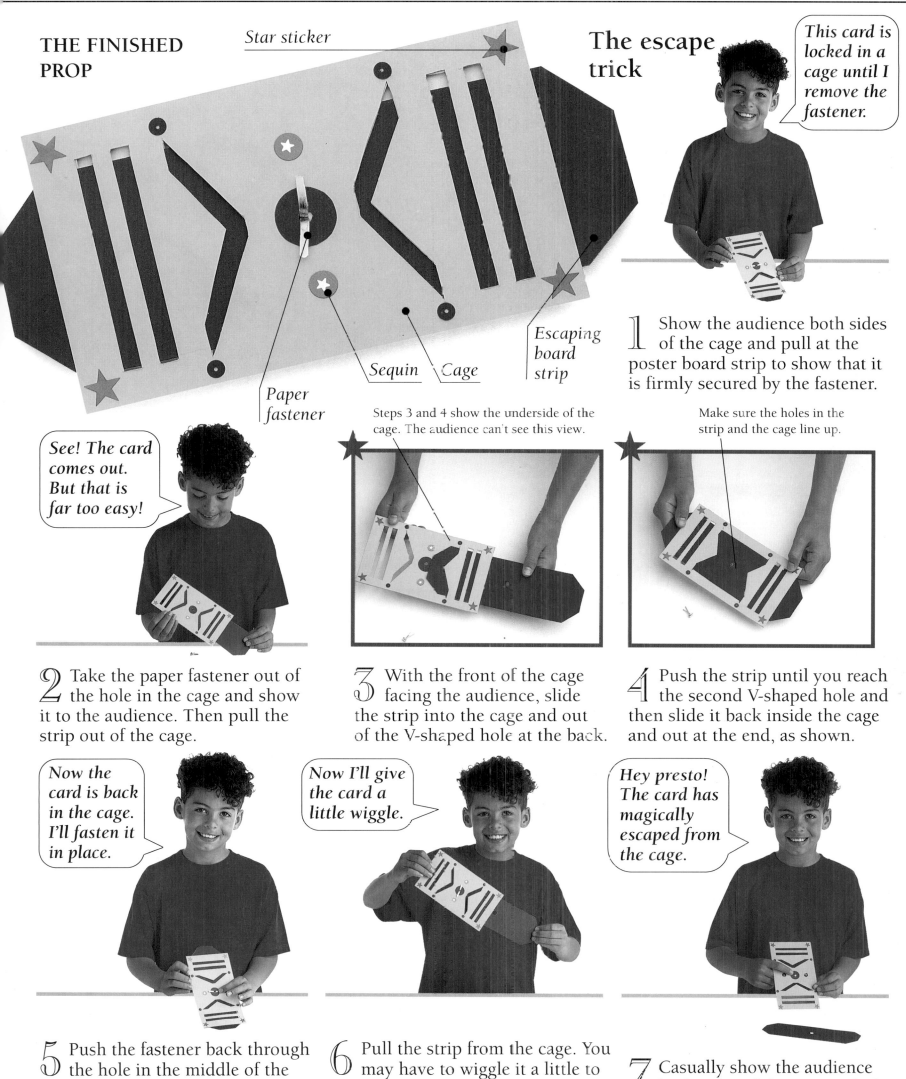

This card is locked in a cage until I remove the fastener.

Paper fastener

Sequin **Cage**

Escaping board strip

1 Show the audience both sides of the cage and pull at the poster board strip to show that it is firmly secured by the fastener.

See! The card comes out. But that is far too easy!

Steps 3 and 4 show the underside of the cage. The audience can't see this view.

Make sure the holes in the strip and the cage line up.

2 Take the paper fastener out of the hole in the cage and show it to the audience. Then pull the strip out of the cage.

3 With the front of the cage facing the audience, slide the strip into the cage and out of the V-shaped hole at the back.

4 Push the strip until you reach the second V-shaped hole and then slide it back inside the cage and out at the end, as shown.

Now the card is back in the cage. I'll fasten it in place.

Now I'll give the card a little wiggle.

Hey presto! The card has magically escaped from the cage.

5 Push the fastener back through the hole in the middle of the cage, from the back to the front. Fold the legs of the fastener flat.

6 Pull the strip from the cage. You may have to wiggle it a little to make the hole in the strip pass over the head of the fastener.

7 Casually show the audience both sides of the cage with the fastener still firmly in place.

27

CURIOUS COINS

Try to untangle this problem! Two colorful strings are tied around a chopstick. Then six coins are threaded onto the strings and tied securely to the chopstick. But incredibly, when the chopstick is removed and the strings pulled tight, the coins fly off the rope and the knot magically disappears.

EQUIPMENT

Compass

Scissors

Felt-tip pen

Pencil

Tape   Craft knife

You will need

Strong glue

Chopstick

Gold poster board

6 ft. (2 m) of thin, colored rope

Chopstick

Decorate the coins with pretend Chinese characters.

Two 3 ft. (1 m) lengths of rope

Making the props

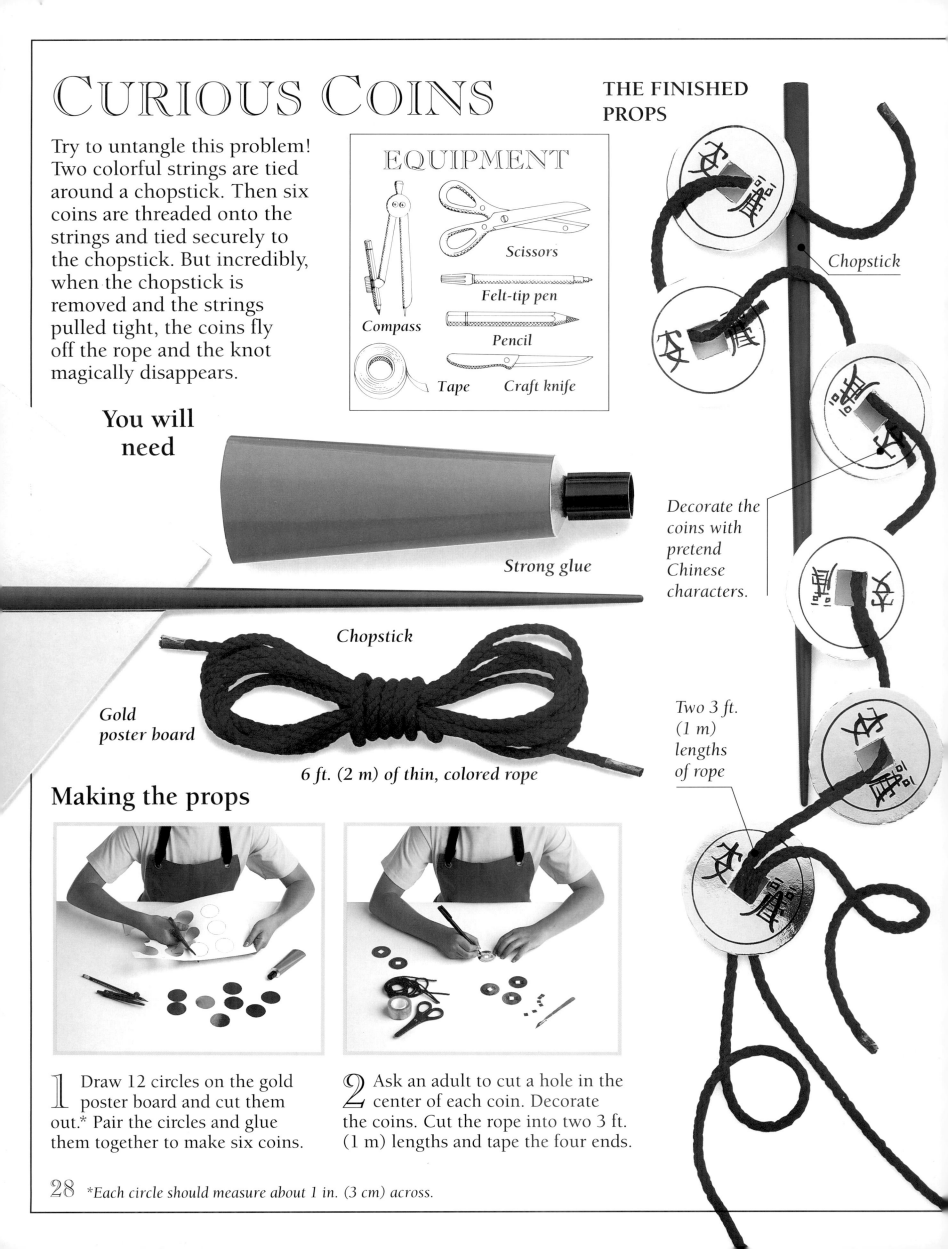

1 Draw 12 circles on the gold poster board and cut them out.* Pair the circles and glue them together to make six coins.

2 Ask an adult to cut a hole in the center of each coin. Decorate the coins. Cut the rope into two 3 ft. (1 m) lengths and tape the four ends.

28 *Each circle should measure about 1 in. (3 cm) across.

Curious coin trick

This is a mystery from the Far East.

First the strings need to be tied together.

Then the coins are threaded on.

Lay out the coins.

1 Ask someone in your audience to hold the chopstick in the air. Hang the ropes over the chopstick, as shown.

2 Take one set of ropes in each hand and tie them in a single knot below the chopstick, as shown. Pull the knot tight.

3 Thread three coins onto each set of strings, as shown. Then give the two sets of ends to your assistant to hold.

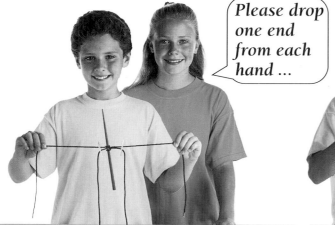

Please drop one end from each hand ...

... so I can tie a knot.

4 Ask your assistant to drop one string from each hand, so that one end hangs on either side of the chopstick, as shown.

5 Take the two dropped strings and tie them in a single knot. Give the two ends back to your assistant to hold.

6 Ask your assistant to hold the strings loosely. (The string must be slack.) Then slowly pull out the chopstick.

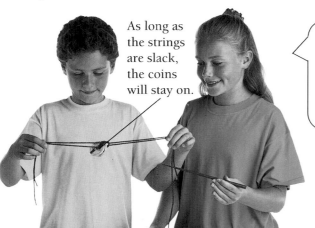

As long as the strings are slack, the coins will stay on.

When I shout "GO," pull the strings tight and the knot will disappear.

The knot has disappeared.

7 Make sure the strings are kept slack, as shown. Then tell your assistant to pull the strings tight when you shout "GO!"

8 When the strings are pulled tight, the coins will fly off into the air, much to your assistant's astonishment.

29

PARTY HAT

In this trick, sheets of tissue paper are torn into little pieces and then magically put back together again to make a party hat – much to the surprise of the audience. The hat is hidden in a secret pocket in one of the sheets of tissue paper and during the performance, the torn pieces of tissue are scrunched together to form a colorful rosette, stuck on the front of the hat.

You will need

A sheet of blue tissue paper

A sheet of red tissue paper

Glue stick

THE FINISHED PARTY HAT

Make sure that the hat you make is big enough to fit on your head! And remember to glue the hat into the secret pocket or the rosette will fall off and spoil the trick.

Red and blue tissue paper rosette

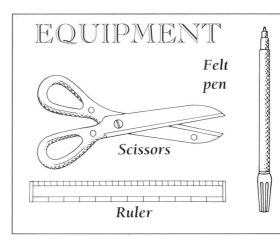

EQUIPMENT

Felt pen

Scissors

Ruler

Making the hat

1 Cut a 12 x 12 in. (30 x 30 cm) square of red tissue. Fold it in half. Glue the two short sides and decorate it with blue tissue strips.

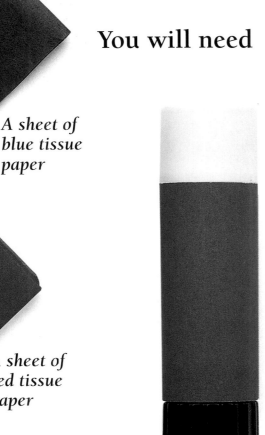

2 Fold the hat in half lengthwise, then fold it in half from side to side, as shown. Fold the hat side to side once again.

The secret pocket

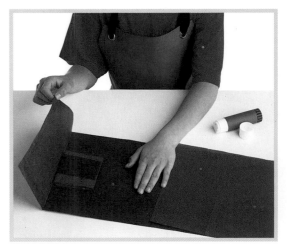

3 Glue the hat to the blue tissue paper.* Fold the paper over the hat, then glue the edges of the flap and stick them down.

30

Use a small dab of glue to do this.

The torn tissue hat trick

Here are two sheets of tissue paper: one blue and one red.

Now I'm going to tear them in half ...

Don't stand in front of a bright light, or the audience will spot the secret pocket.

Scrunch the hidden pocket in your hand.

Red tissue paper hat with a blue tissue paper stripe

1 Take one sheet in each hand and put the blue sheet behind the red sheet, so that the secret pocket cannot be seen.

2 Hold the two sheets as shown, and then tear them in half. Don't worry about tearing neatly.

... and in half again.

That's enough tearing for now.

3 Move the torn pieces to the front and tear the sheets in half again. Move the torn pieces to the front once more.

4 Then, tear open the secret pocket at the back. You can see the hat now, but don't worry – the audience can't.

5 Move the piece of tissue paper that formed the back of the pocket to the front of the pile, as shown.

Now I'll make a magic package.

8 Now you can put on the hat. The audience will wonder where it came from.

And presto – a magic hat!

6 Then, using both hands, crush the torn tissue paper pieces into the middle, and squash the edges of the hat around them.

7 Then, holding the rosette in one hand, gently unfold the hat. (The torn pieces stay squashed together to form the rosette.)

MAGIC BOX

With the help of this magical box, you will be able to baffle your friends when you make objects appear out of thin air! The secret behind the trick is a black felt bag hidden in the lid of the box and brimming with treasure. Below, you can find out how to make the box, then turn the page to learn how to perform this amazing piece of magic.

A black felt square for the bag

Colored paper to cover and line the box

You will need

Clear fishing line or thread

Star sequins

Strong glue

Lots of small sequins

Large sequins

Star stickers

EQUIPMENT

Pencil   Scissors

Needle   Ruler

A shoe box

32

What to do

Lots of colored ribbon

1 Draw around all the sides of the box and lid on black paper and cut out the pieces. Use these to line the insides of the box and lid.

2 To make the bag, fold the felt square in half and glue the two short sides together. Sew a long piece of thread into one top corner.

3 Ask an adult to make two holes in the front of the lid, where shown. Sew the bag into the lid so that it hangs freely, as shown.*

4 To cover the magic box, draw around all of the sides of the box and lid on colored paper, as shown. Cut the pieces out.

5 Fold the pieces around the box and lid. Carefully glue the paper around the box, then neatly trim the edges.

6 Decorate the magic box with ribbon and sequins. The lid must be particularly spectacular to draw the audience's attention.

We have used red thread so you can see what to do, but you must use clear thread instead.

33

Box Of Tricks

And here is the finished magic box. Everyone can see that the box is completely empty, and yet you can reach into it and pull out lots of surprises. You can use the box to make things vanish, too – just reverse the actions shown below. Practice the moves in front of a mirror to make sure that your audience can't see the hidden bag.

Colored ribbons

PACKING YOUR BAG

Before you start to perform the trick, you will need to pack the felt bag. It is best to fill it with small things, like sequins, stars, and candies. Here are some of the things we used.

Star sequins

Chocolate coins

Ropes

The big box trick

Preparation

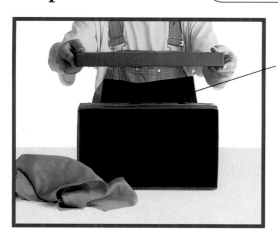

The secret bag hangs down behind the box.

> On my birthday, a magician sent me this mysterious box.

> He said it was full of treasure if I followed his instructions.

Put the box on its side and place the lid on top of the box, as shown, with the bag hanging behind the bottom of the box.

1 Place the magic box in front of you on the table, as shown. Show the audience that the box is completely empty.

2 Lift the back of the lid up with both hands, until the top of the lid is facing your audience. Don't lift the front of the lid at all.

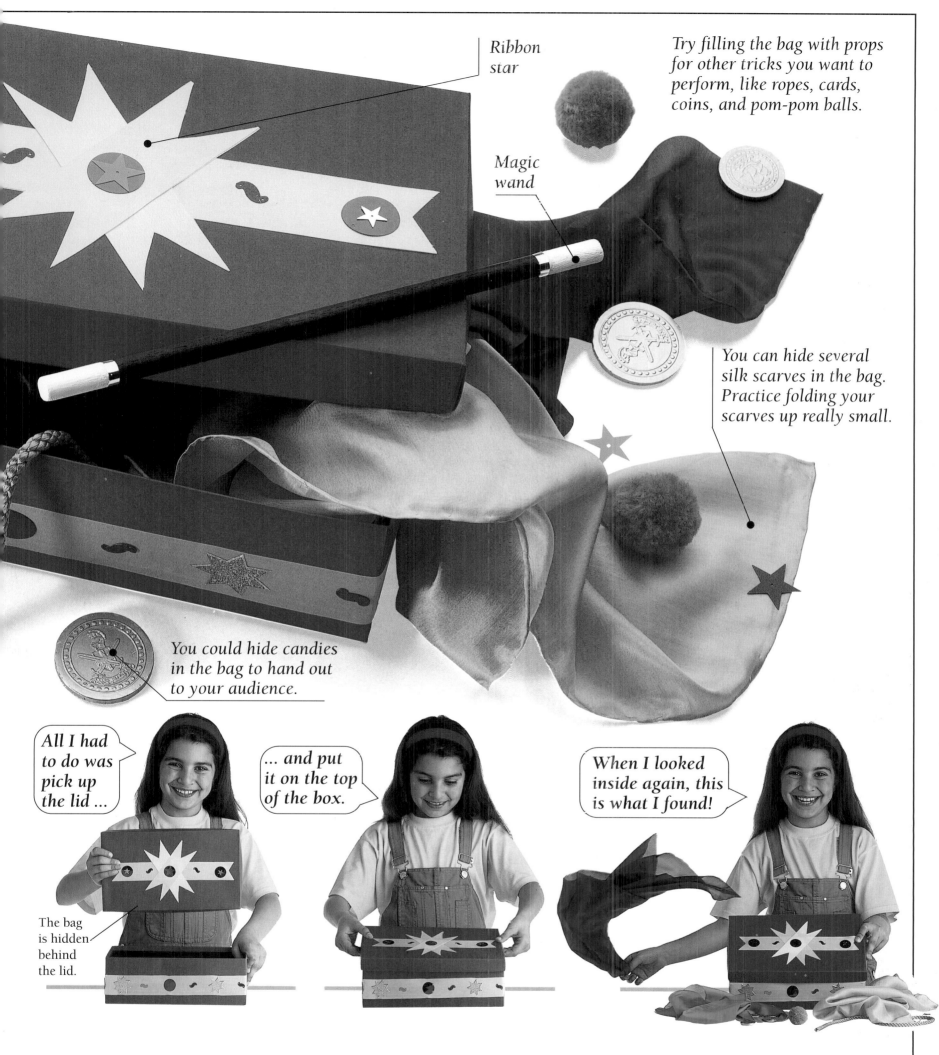

Ribbon star

Try filling the bag with props for other tricks you want to perform, like ropes, cards, coins, and pom-pom balls.

Magic wand

You can hide several silk scarves in the bag. Practice folding your scarves up really small.

You could hide candies in the bag to hand out to your audience.

All I had to do was pick up the lid ...

The bag is hidden behind the lid.

... and put it on the top of the box.

When I looked inside again, this is what I found!

3 Keep the lid facing the audience with one hand, and use your other hand to place the box flat on the table.

4 Put the front edge of the lid in front of the box, and tip the lid back until the bag falls into the box. Put the lid down flat.

5 Lift up the back of the lid with one hand. Reach into the bag with the other hand and, one by one, pull out all the treasures.

UNEQUAL ROPES

In this classic rope trick, three different ropes magically become the same length. Then, just as quickly, the ropes change back to their different lengths. Color code the ends of your ropes to help you practice this trick, but perform the trick with ropes of the same color.

You will need

These three ropes are very strange. At the moment they are different lengths.

1 Show the ropes to the audience one by one. Hold them in your hand as shown, with the shortest rope in the middle.

EQUIPMENT

Felt-tip pen

Scissors

Ruler

5¹/₂ ft. (2 m) of rope

Colored tape

What to do

1 Cut three lengths of rope, one 35 in. (90 cm) long, one 22 in. (55 cm) long, and one 8 in. (20 cm) long.

2 To help you practice the trick, give each rope different colored ends – short rope (blue), middle rope (yellow), and long rope (green).*

4 Take the end of the long rope (green) and place it next to the other green end. Put the free yellow end next to the green ends.

Now they're all the same size!

7 When the ends are pulled apart, the ropes will seem to be the same length. Let the one yellow and two green ends hang down.

* Remember the ends must all be the same color when you perform the trick.

2 With your other hand, reach behind the long rope and take hold of the end of the short rope (with blue ends), as shown.

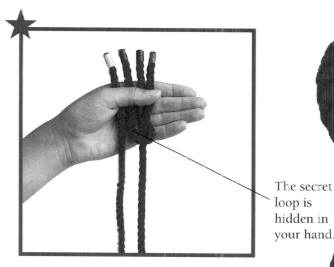

3 Bring the blue end around in front of the long rope and up next to the yellow end, forming a secret loop.

The secret loop is hidden in your hand.

THE FINISHED ROPES

Long rope with green ends

Short rope with blue ends

Medium rope with yellow ends

Keep the backs of your hands toward the audience at all times.

But sometimes they behave very oddly ...

... and they start to change length.

This hand is hiding the secret loop.

5 Split the ends into two sets of three, as shown. A yellow and two blues in one hand, and two greens and a yellow in the other.

6 Make the ropes shake in your hand, then take one group in each hand and **slowly** pull your hands apart, as shown.

But they soon become bored with the game and change back to their normal lengths.

8 Bundle all the ropes together into one hand, as shown. Take hold of any end and slowly pull a rope from your hand.

9 Pull out the other ropes in the same way and show them to the audience. Incredibly, all three ropes are different lengths again.

PUZZLING PICTURES

Sensational is the only word for this trick. An empty scrapbook magically becomes full of pictures – with just a flick of the wrist. You can make a scrapbook by folding sheets of paper in half, one inside the other, to make pages. Fold a different color sheet for a cover. Staple through the folds to hold the book together. Practice this trick in front of a mirror so that you can flip through the book without fumbling.

You will need

Colored paper

Scrapbook

Glue stick

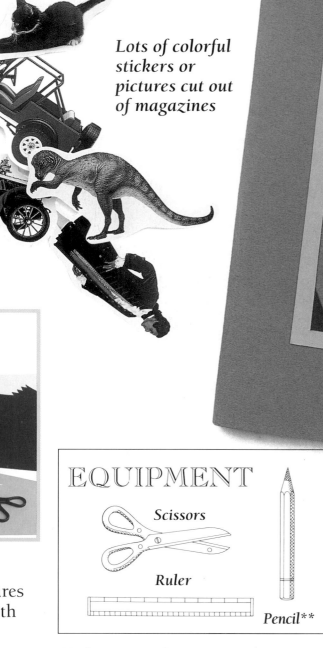

Lots of colorful stickers or pictures cut out of magazines

Preparing the scrapbook

1 Leave the first page and every other spread* blank. Cut the top corner off the right-hand page of every blank spread, as shown.

2 Stick pictures on the first spread of two pages and every other spread. Cut the bottom-right corner off every picture spread.

3 Decorate the front of the scrapbook with more pictures and stickers. Make a border with colored paper.

*A spread is the name given to the facing left- and right-hand pages of an open book.

EQUIPMENT

Scissors

Ruler

*Pencil***

** If you are making your own scrapbook, you will need a stapler, too.

Red paper shapes

The magic scrapbook trick

I use this scrapbook to show people my hobby.

Sticker

Yellow paper border

1 Show the scrapbook to the audience. Hold the book with your thumb at the bottom corner, ready to flip through the pages.

At first they can't guess what my hobby is.

2 Flip through the pages of the scrapbook from front to back, using your thumb, as shown. The pages will all appear to be empty.

But they soon see – it's magic!

THE FINISHED SCRAPBOOK

Here is the finished scrapbook. After the first blank page, the picture spreads and the blank spreads alternate, so that each picture spread is followed by a blank spread throughout the book.

3 Move your hand to the top corner of the book and flip through the book again. All the pages will magically appear full.

ODD CARD OUT

All magicians are expected to perform card tricks, and this one is very clever. You ask a friend to pick a card, then, when you shuffle though the pack, your friend will discover that he has chosen the only odd card! This trick needs lots of practice, as you must handle the cards very smoothly if you are to deceive your friend.

You will need

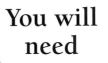

Poster paints

Thick paper

EQUIPMENT

Paintbrush

Scissors

Saucer

Jar of water   **Pencil**

Ruler   **Compass**

Making the cards

1 Draw 12 rectangles on paper. Draw a circle on six rectangles and a triangle on the others. Cut out the rectangles to make 12 cards.

2 Paint the circles red and the triangles green. Then draw the same design on the back of all the cards and color it in with paint.

CUTTING THE CARDS

Before you start the trick, you will need to sort the cards so that a red card is always followed by a green card all the way through the pack. With the red and green cards set up like this, you can cut the cards as often as you like and the order will stay the same.

Green triangle card

Red spot card

The backs of the cards have a colorful design.

Odd card out trick

Please choose a card.

Put your card down on the table without looking at it.

I'll just put the pack back together.

1 Fan the cards out in your hands, with the backs of the cards showing. Ask a spectator to choose one of the cards.

2 Separate the cards at the card that the spectator chooses. Ask him to take his chosen card and put it facedown on the table.

3 Place all the cards that were on top of the chosen card underneath the rest of the pack. Square up the edges of the cards.

I'll show you the rest of the cards.

4 Hold the cards in one hand and take the top card off the pile with the other hand, as shown.

5 Without changing your grip, turn both hands over from your wrists, as shown, to show two cards of the same pattern.

All these cards are the same.

The audience will see cards of the same pattern each time.

6 Turn both hands over, and put the single card facedown on the table. Take the top card off the pack and put it on top of the card on the table.

7 Repeat steps 5 and 6 with the rest of the cards in your hand. Ask the spectator to turn over the chosen card and watch the surprise on his face when he realizes it's the odd one out.

Please take a look at your card. You chose the odd one out!

MIND-READING ACT

Wouldn't it be useful if you could read other people's minds? Well, with this trick your friends will believe you can do just that – when you correctly predict the color of a card they have chosen in secret. Try to act the part of a mysterious mind reader – it will convince the audience of your amazing powers!

EQUIPMENT

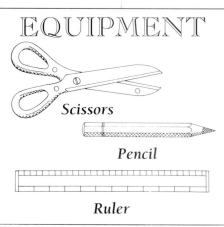

Scissors

Pencil

Ruler

You will need

Strong glue

Colored paper

Elastic

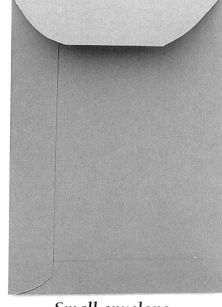

Small envelope

Tape

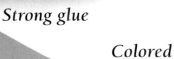

Clipboard with a large double-sided clip

White cardboard

Felt-tip pens

Making the clipboard

1 Stretch two strips of elastic around the clipboard. Glue the ends of each strip together. Divide each strip into four card pockets with pieces of tape, as shown.

2 Decorate the back of the board and the small envelope with colored paper cutouts. Glue the cutouts in position.

3 Cut out nine cards (each no wider than the clip on the board). Color three-quarters of eight cards red, and one quarter* of each another color. Number them 1 to 8. Make the last card red all over.

*The colored quarter must be completely covered when the card is put under the clip.

Preparation

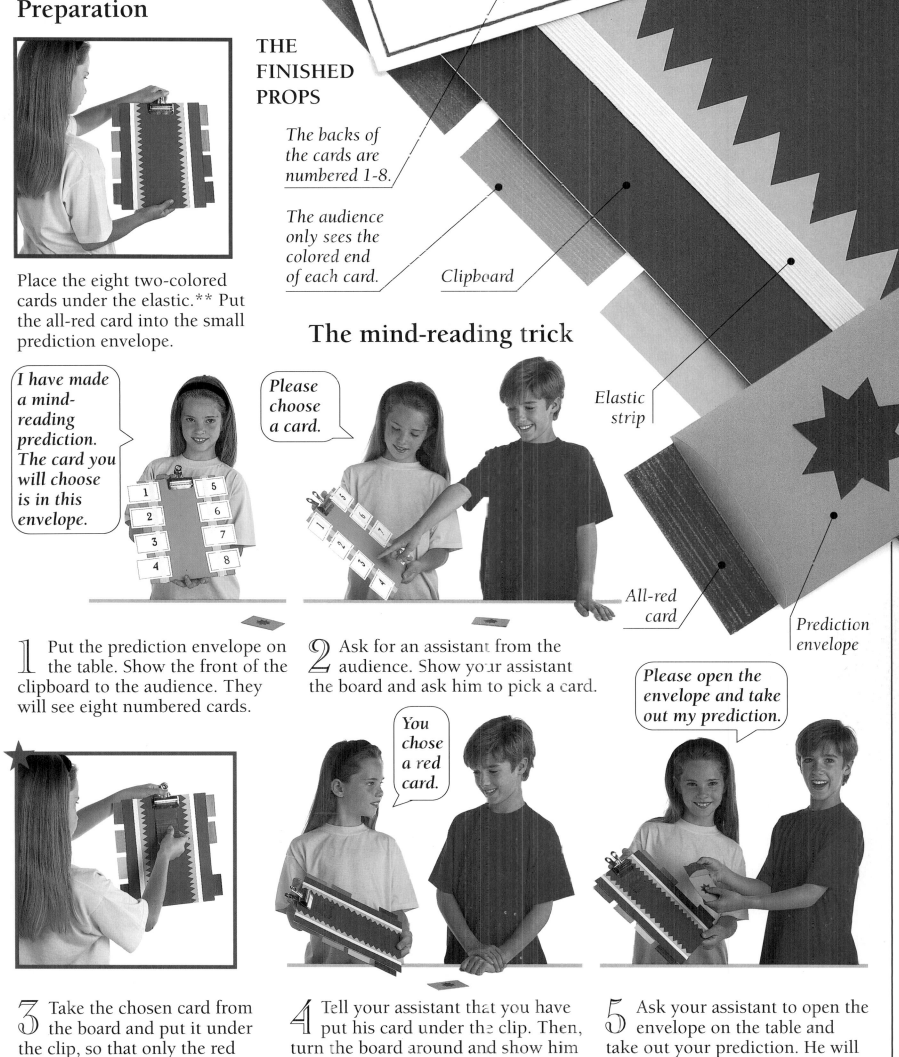

Place the eight two-colored cards under the elastic.** Put the all-red card into the small prediction envelope.

THE FINISHED PROPS

The backs of the cards are numbered 1-8.

The audience only sees the colored end of each card.

Clipboard

Elastic strip

All-red card

Prediction envelope

The mind-reading trick

I have made a mind-reading prediction. The card you will choose is in this envelope.

Please choose a card.

1   Put the prediction envelope on the table. Show the front of the clipboard to the audience. They will see eight numbered cards.

2   Ask for an assistant from the audience. Show your assistant the board and ask him to pick a card.

You chose a red card.

Please open the envelope and take out my prediction.

3   Take the chosen card from the board and put it under the clip, so that only the red part of the card is showing.

**Make sure that the red part of each card is hidden by the clipboard.

4   Tell your assistant that you have put his card under the clip. Then, turn the board around and show him that he has chosen the red card.

5   Ask your assistant to open the envelope on the table and take out your prediction. He will be amazed that you were right.

43

LEVITATING CARD

An important rule of magic is to never reveal the secrets of your tricks – but at the end of this trick, that is exactly what you do. The audience won't believe their eyes as they see a card rise out of an envelope and float in midair. But their surprise will turn to laughter when you "accidentally" reveal the secret.

Before you start, stick a piece of double-sided tape to one end of your magic wand, and trim off the edges. When you perform, make sure that your audience is in front of you; this way no one will see you cheating until the end.

You will need

Large envelope

EQUIPMENT

Paintbrush

Saucer

Jar of water

Pencil

Double-sided tape

Ruler

Scissors

Poster paints

Star sequins and star stickers

Colored paper

Thick yellow paper

Magic wand (See page 6)

Making the props

1 Cut out three rectangular cards of thick paper just smaller than your envelope. Paint a different symbol on each card.

2 Cut a large rectangular hole out of the back of the envelope, as shown. Decorate the front of the envelope with stars and paper.

The levitating card trick

I'm going to show you an amazing illusion with cards.

Please pick a card.

1 Place the cards on the table. Then pick up the wand so that the sticky end is in your hand. Use the wand to point to the cards.

2 Put the wand under your arm (the sticky end should point toward the audience). Ask a spectator to choose a card.

Make sure the audience doesn't see the back of the envelope.

Watch – your card will rise out of the envelope.

Press the envelope firmly against the end of the wand.

3 Pick up all the cards face-up, putting the chosen card on the bottom of the pile. Put the cards face forward into the envelope.

4 Bring the envelope up and press the cards against the sticky end of the wand, through the hole in the envelope.

Amazing! Your card is floating in thin air.

Thank you. Thank you.

THE FINISHED PROPS
Decorate the front of the envelope with colored paper cutouts and a few stars.

5 Slowly pull the envelope down and off the card. Then wave your hands around the card so that it appears to be floating in midair.

6 Now take a bow. The audience will see the card stuck to the wand. Everyone will laugh when they see how they've been fooled.

FOOLING A FRIEND

These two quick challenges will trick your friends. First, ask them to tie a knot in a piece of rope without letting go of the ends – and watch as they tie themselves up in knots! Then give them the five-card challenge – it turns out to be much harder than it looks!

You will need

Poster board

Strong glue

Star stickers

Paper clip

About 3 ft. (1 m) of rope

The impossible knot

This is how you tie the knot.

I'm still holding the ends.

Look! A knot has appeared.

A loop forms over your hand.

1 Put the rope on the table. Fold your arms and pick up an end of the rope in each hand, as shown.

2 Slowly unfold your arms while keeping a tight hold on the ends. Shake the loop that forms forward and off your hand.

3 When the loop has fallen off your hand, pull your arms out straight. A knot will form in the middle of the rope.

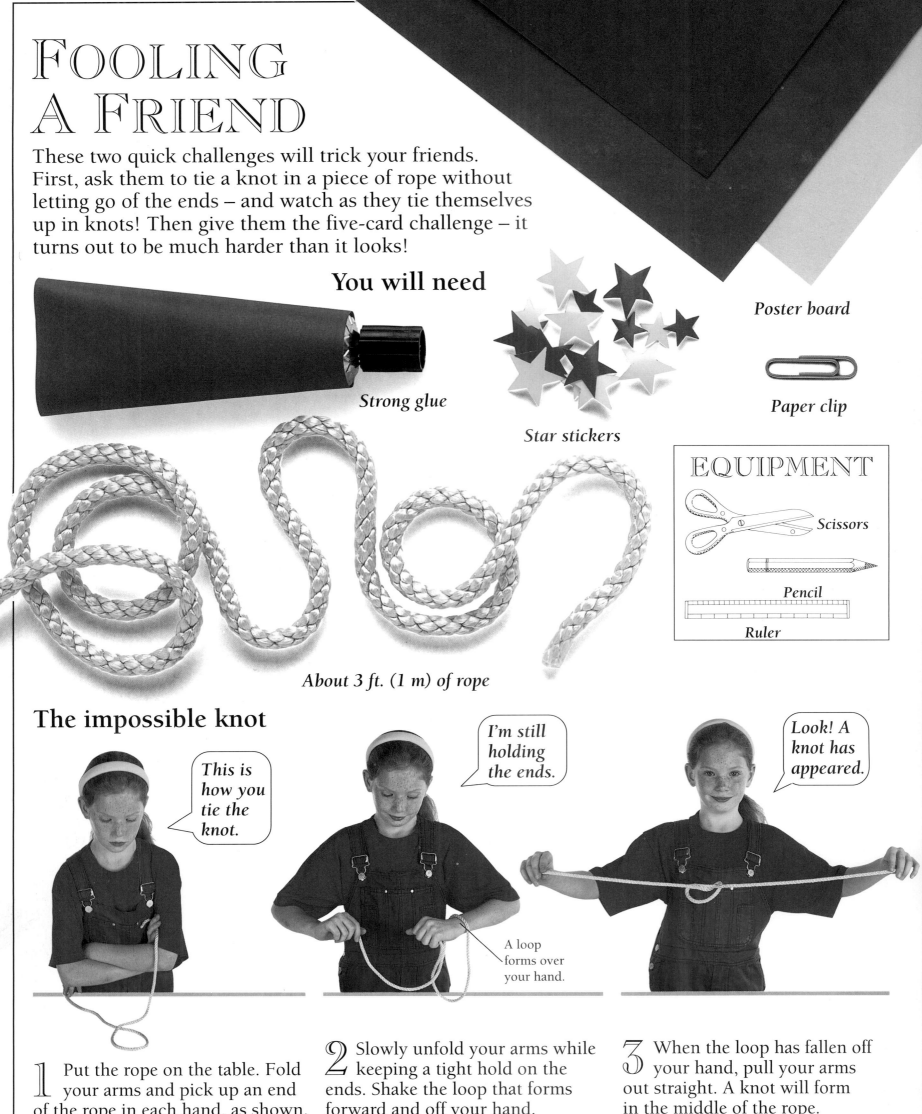

Making the card trick

1 Draw five rectangles on both yellow and blue poster board. Cut them out. Glue each blue card to a yellow one.

2 Stick different numbers of yellow stars on the (blue) fronts of four of the cards, and a few red stars on the front of the last card.

3 Decorate the card backs so that each is identical. Glue the cards together in a row, with the card with red stars in the middle.

The fan trick

Before you start this trick, put the paper clip on the card with red stars, in the middle of the row.

Blue card fronts

Paper clip

Red star sticker

The middle card must look different from the others.

Yellow star sticker

When I turn these cards over, try to put the paper clip on the card with red stars.

No! It's not as easy as you think.

1 Show a friend the row of cards with the blue sides showing. Ask your friend to remove the paper clip.

Paper clip

2 Turn the row of cards over so that the backs are showing, then ask your friend to slide the paper clip onto the same red card.

Paper clip

3 Turn the cards over again to see if your friend has chosen the right card. He will be surprised at how badly he guessed.

TIPS FOR TRICKS

The most important rule when performing magic is that it should be FUN. You want your audience to enjoy themselves.

★

Don't perform a trick more than once to the same audience.

★

When you finish a trick, put the props away. It is very important that you keep your magic secrets to yourself.

★

Practice each trick before you perform it so that your moves appear smooth and natural.

★

Rehearse each trick in front of a mirror so you can see the view that the audience will see.

★

Rehearse your lines at the same time as your trick. Remember, what you say is just as important as what you do. Our suggested lines are only guidelines. You will soon develop a script of your own.

★

Always keep your magic props clean and in good condition.

★

Be confident, relaxed, and have fun when you perform.

★

Good Luck!